Be Still

Presented to

_____

By

_____

On

_____

a Sit for a Bit book

Be Still

written by **Kathryn O'Brien** illustrated by **Gillian Flint**

Tyndale House Publishers, Inc.
Carol Stream, Illinois

Visit Tyndale's website for kids at www.tyndale.com/kids.

TYNDALE is a registered trademark of Tyndale House Publishers, Inc. The Tyndale Kids logo is a trademark of Tyndale House Publishers, Inc.

Be Still

Designed by Jacqueline L. Nuñez

Edited by Stephanie Rische

Published in association with the literary agency of D.C. Jacobson & Associates LLC, an Author Management Company. www.dcjacobson.com.

For manufacturing information regarding this product, please call 1-800-323-9400.

ISBN 978-1-4964-1116-7

Printed in China

22	21	20	19	18	17	16
7	6	5	4	3	2	1

A Note to Parents

Dear Parents,

As believers, we are called to know God's Word—to hide it and hold it in our hearts. What a wonderful opportunity and an awesome responsibility we have to share His Word, teach His life-changing promises, and impart His powerful truths to our children. My prayer is that God uses this book to help children learn, understand, and indeed hold God's Word in their little hearts for a lifetime.

—Kathryn O'Brien

The grass withers and the flowers fade,
but the word of our God stands forever.

Isaiah 40:8

1

Be

2

Be kind.

Be silly!

Be a friend.

Be yourself.

Be still

Shhhh. Slow down.

Take a breath.

No hurrying or scurrying or worrying.

No wanting or whining.

No fussing. No rushing.

Safe and still.

Be still, and

And peaceful.

And quiet.

And calm.

Ahhhh.

Be still, and

know

Know My joy when you obey.

Know My grace when you don't.

Know My Word.

Know Me.

Be still, and

know that

That you are safe.

That you are loved.

That you are always on My mind.

That I will never leave you.

I see you.

I hear you.

I know you.

I love you.

Be still, and

know that
I am

I am real.

I am good.

I am patient.

I am with you.

I am the great I AM.

Be still, and

know that I am God!

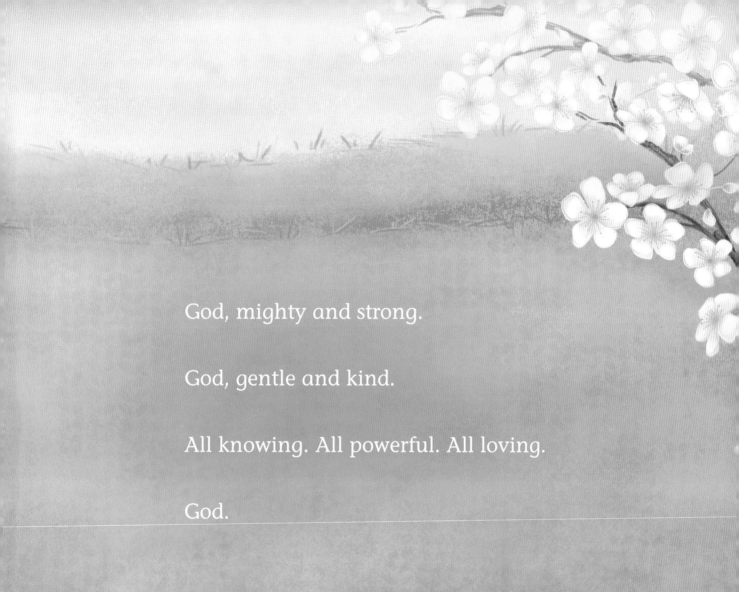

God, mighty and strong.

God, gentle and kind.

All knowing. All powerful. All loving.

God.

Be still, and know that I am God!

Psalm 46:10

34

For Alyse

It roared a great roar of victory
as Dream Dragon limped to the edge
of the boy's mind where
it faded then disappeared.

For four sleeps T-Rex was the
boy's main dream.
He fought off bad dreams as ferociously
as Dream Dragon.

T-Rex was not only big and strong.

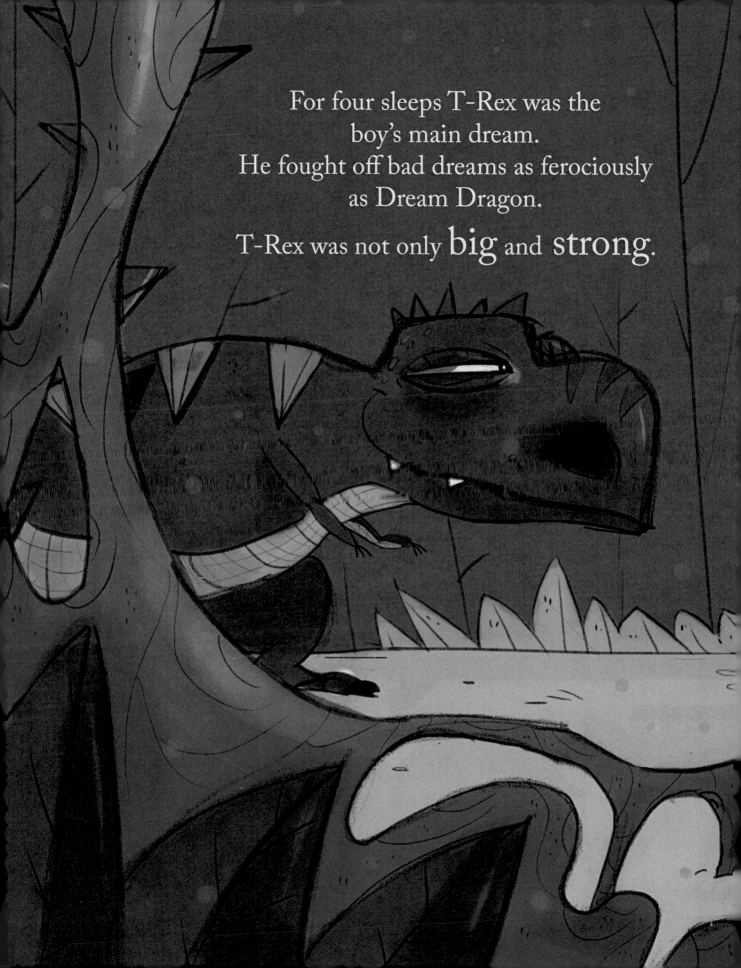

He was a hunter.
He could track a ghost
through a haunted forest.

He could **spot** a monster
on a distant mountain.

He could **smell** a creepy-crawly-scary-thing
hiding in a swamp.

No bad dreams stood a chance
while he was there.

But, on the fifth night,
T-Rex was defeated by a super hero.

A few sleeps after that,
a pirate made super hero walk the plank.

The boy **never** dreamed about

Dream Dragon again

But

one night ...

The girl was tucked up
in bed, dreaming.

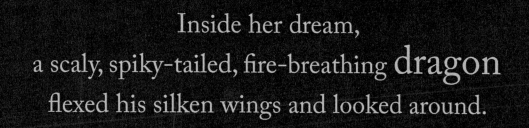

Inside her dream,
a scaly, spiky-tailed, fire-breathing dragon
flexed his silken wings and looked around.

THE END

38430488R00020

Made in the USA
San Bernardino, CA
10 June 2019

Dream Dragon wanted to be the main dream, the one that would be remembered in the morning. He knew that other dreams would try to take his place. As soon as they appeared, he pounced.

As quick as a heartbeat.
As sudden as a sneeze.

He chased nice dreams to the edge of
the boy's mind where they floated
around out of his way.
But whenever a scary dream appeared,
he scorched its hide with hot flame.

"GET OUT OF HERE!" he roared.
"DON'T FRIGHTEN MY BOY!"
The boy's bad dreams melted in fear.

For three sleeps Dream Dragon was the main dream.
But on the fourth night,
a dream egg appeared in the boy's mind.
Dream Dragon moved closer.

The egg was so big.
Whatever was inside would be big.
He hoped it was just a giant fluffy duck.
He would only have to say **"BOO!"**
to a giant fluffy duck
and it would run away.

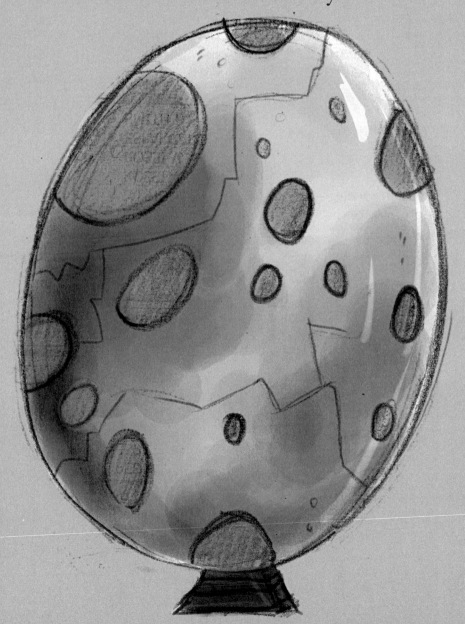

Dream Dragon was scared, but he was also brave. **"THIS EGG MIGHT CONTAIN A VERY BIG BAD DREAM,"** he said.

"IF IT IS A VERY BIG BAD DREAM,
I MUST GET RID OF IT."

Two glowing red eyes peered at him
through a crack in the top of the egg.
A muscly leg broke through one side of the egg.

Another muscly leg broke through the other side.
A thick tail burst through the back of the egg.
Then a mighty body shattered the shell
into a million pieces.

CRACK
CRACK

Dream Dragon stared up, and up, and up
at the boy's new dream.
It was a **ferocious** creature the boy
had learned about in school that day.

CHOMP

A set of sharp teeth sank
into Dream Dragon's hide.

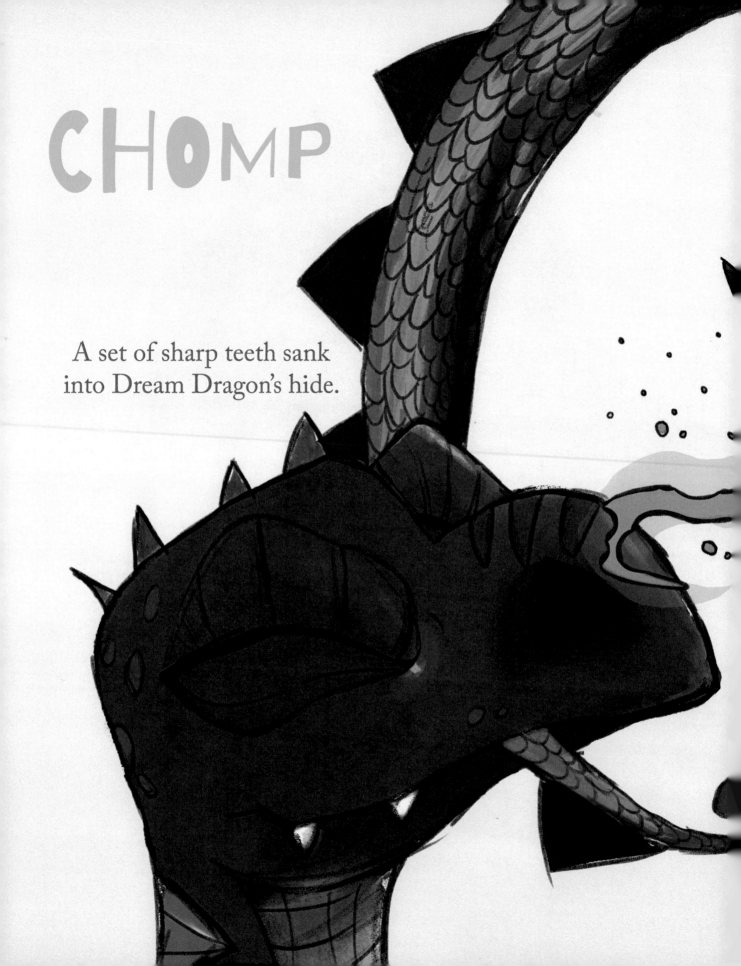

WHOOSH

Dream Dragon fired a burst of flame.

Dream Dragon fought long.

Dream Dragon fought hard.

But the new dream was too strong.

SOB